Eros: Of H
and Heartfelt Things

Christy Ng Yenyi

Presentation by *BookLeaf Publishing*

Web: www.bookleafpub.com

E-mail: info@bookleafpub.com

ISBN: 9789358319279

First edition 2024

DEDICATION

To the 14-year-old Christy that began this whole "poetry" venture - we did it.

To the past crushes and unintentional heartbreakers...

To the real love stories witnessed and shared by those I have encountered...

To the Hollywood romcoms and Korean dramas...

- Thank you for being the sources of inspiration for the writings in this book.

Most importantly, to God who blessed me with the gift of emotion and writing.

ACKNOWLEDGEMENT

Thank you to the publisher for reviving an interest once thought lost in adulthood and for making a secret dream first formed in adolescence come true - I get to formally call myself a poet now because of you, and a published poet at that.

Teenage me did not foresee that adult me would end up having a published book to call her own, nor did she think that it would ever be possible to get her work out in the real world - she just did not know how, but here we are. Here's to all those involved with turning wishful thinking into actualised reality – you are the real MVP.

PREFACE

"Eros" - the Greek term used to capture the type of love relating to romantic feelings and relationships. And with romance, comes the bitter and the sweet.

This book explores the use of pure and innocent language in expressing these two sides to Eros. With the poet's intention to write from a place of detached intimacy, sources of inspiration were intertwined and written in the first-person to create the "main character" effect for her readers - "Hey you, this world is actually yours."

My Prince, My Soulmate, My Friend

You ran over whenever I needed a hand,
Whenever I needed a laugh, giggle or smile,
You took the journey over sky, sea and land,
Whenever I needed company, even for a little while.

You became someone special whose love and care,
Felt like home whether we were far apart or near,
I treasure you dearly for you are a find so rare,
You ended my search for love after all these years.

You gave me courage to face my deepest fears,
All of my burdens and worries only to you I bare,
When times were rough, you brought me cheer,
Such comfort comes when by my side you are there.

The showers of support that you constantly
bring,
Never seem to pose warning signs of a dead end,
In the words of Monica's vow to Chandler Bing,
I found in you "my prince, my soulmate, my
friend".

Being Fooled

I treated you like royalty, an emperor no less a king,
We shared in dance, in laughter we sing,
I counted the days whenever we would cling,
I thought I meant a lot to you, a special something.

But out of your life, like a jester, a fool, I got fling,
I crashed from the clouds since you've cut off my wings,
To be yours, I blindly committed my everything,
For your love, for your heart, that special ring.

And now I'm left with a heart constantly in aching,
Being played for a fool, my heart went breaking,
As I lost all happiness, my voice began cracking,
This heart of mine left broken open and tearing.

Too Shy A Confession

You often glanced back at me with your caring eyes,
Yet you barely utter a word, I wonder why,
But still I'm filled with warmth whenever you're nearby,
Perhaps it's the safety I feel being by your side.

You seem like the perfect complement to me,
Your presence like rays of light when I'm gloomy,
It's true, your smile shines brighter than the sun,
While watching out for flags of red, I found none.

I wonder what it would be like to call you mine,
But I fumble with my words all the time,
You might not notice how I am extremely shy,
I wish I knew how to carry on beyond saying "Hi".

Perhaps in time, I'll find the boldness to confess,
One day I'll muster up the courage to let it off my chest,
But for now, I'd settle with admiring you from afar,
And spotting you from the crowd wherever you are.

If Only

If only you could've seen how my heart beats,
I know you wouldn't have thought to leave,
But now there you go, you're off with your feet,
And now I'm filled with regret, can't take the heat.

If only you could've stayed for a little while longer,
I know this love would've grown a lot stronger,
But now with another, you're getting closer,
I knew I should've talked with you a lot sooner.

If only you could've given your eyes time to see,
I know you would've seen the bond you shared with me,
We would've worked to make it work, you see,
But now with another, your heart will forever be.

My Guardian Angel

Nightmares of the past had left me with
lingering pain,
Left me wondering if love was nothing but pure
vain,
But life had a way of bringing a rainbow after
the rain,
Showed me that love had far more for me to
gain.

In you marched as my immediate bodyguard,
Started taking note of who had my best interests
at heart,
Those who plot evil kept away with time apart,
But time was made for those with good to
impart.

Your eyes ever on the lookout for potential
wreckers,
Your hands ever ready to pull me away from
danger,
Your ears ever on the alert for threats from
strangers,
My guardian angel, could I ever have a better
protector.

Though life had been tough, the road had been rough,
Your love kept me going, always more than enough,
To help me heal, stand tall and not be swept off,
I always knew you were sent from nowhere but above.

Goodbye My Love

As the both of us set off onto our separate ways,
You can trust that I'll never forget those lovely days,
You left a void that makes me fall to my knees,
Since you had left, my life had not been at ease.

You were the best person I had ever come to know,
And now I am here, nothing but a shell, all alone,
Left to wonder of all the possibilities I will miss,
How could I not see the future you pictured with me.

Here's me bidding you farewell and goodbye my love,
Know that I still wish you the best as you rise above,
You never asked but worry not, I'll be alright,
I hide the truth that my dreams are of you every night.

Whatever Happens

No matter how smooth or rough it went each day,
You stayed by my side every step of the way,
Found ways to keep the monsters in my mind away,
The best being watching the sunset by the coastal bay.

Even when I tried to push you far from my side,
You chose a life that made you my forever inner guide,
To show me where I stood when my worlds collide,
And transformed me back into someone dignified.

You constantly checked in to make sure all was okay,
And listened in on the stories that I had to say,
When voices got loud, you called me to your side to lay,
And assured me that by my side, you'll forever stay.

When I felt weakness, you helped me to be
strong,
And helped me see the silver lining behind the
wrongs,
When I wanted to stop, you helped me to carry
on,
And helped me see the light through life’s cons.

Life After You Left

It's been a while since you've rang me up for a call,
Since you've left, I realised I had nothing at all,
Left with no one to lift me when I stumble and fall,
I stay on the ground, I couldn't rise and stand tall.

Life's a misery to be living without you at all,
I wait by the phone, looking out for even a missed call,
I've been waiting to return to the arms I adore,
But now you're truly gone, left a false sense of lull.

My life without you is nothing but a dead-end wall,
Can't turn anywhere, to the ground, I weep and fall,
I realised that I need you to be strong and stand tall,
To be in my life, to hold me together, to be my all.

Love Without Words

The past brought me nothing but tears and cries,
But I promised I won't allow this gentle heart to die,
So I went on a search for someone worth better,
Someone who was worth my penned love letters.

Then you came along with nothing but a blank card,
But I felt Cupid's shot in the bullseye of my heart,
'Cos you showed me more of what truly mattered,
That words didn't matter if actions didn't follow after.

It showed through the way you worked in the silence,
You never failed to show your care in the little actions,
Though I didn't picture myself with one not a writer,
I wouldn't trade you for substitutes of any other.

Funny how actions tell more than words could ever say,
These memories crafted made to last forever and always,
It's in how you consistently showed that I'm treasured,
I forget not deeds meant for a lifetime remembered.

One Last Chance

I hear the people's voices saying that I am blind,
They tell me that for another, I should now find,
That it will help to remove you out of my mind,
But somehow, I can't seem to get you pass that
line.

Why can't I seem to shake it off, to loosen this
bind,
I still keep peering and looking for that little
sign,
That tells me you still think that you are mine,
I call out to you for one last chance is what I'd
like.

Let's return to the days when we stayed in over a
dine,
I could show you that I had passed the finish
line,
That love would be a mountain I no longer
climb,
When I get that one last chance with you one
more time.

Still Able To Love You

We could spend hours pointlessly bickering one another,
It's a pattern I've realised would rise each and every day,
Yet I made a promise that I'll be tied to you forever,
Even with the madness that comes along your way.

And it's because you've captured this heart of mine,
That I vow to remain by your side to soothe the pain,
My presence a remedy for the scars to disappear in time,
Though the voices threaten to claw back up the drain.

So I'll keep repeating that I am still able to love you,
Though the darkness keeps the lights dimmed to a half,
I'll remain as your support no matter what you say or do,
For it is you alone that I chose to be forever in love.

When you're down and out, I'll be your helping hand,
Even when you push me away, my spirit will not break,
Have you not realised that I love you with all that I am,
That I'll fight your battles with you, whatever it takes.

Come Back To Me

The connection we shared was my pride and glory,
And now that it's lost, it's turned nightmare into reality,
I come crawling, begging you to continue our journey,
Is this mania talking that together forever is all I see.

I went looking for distractions to fill my crazy feed,
Just put your trust in me that I'll be everything you need,
Just come back my love and I'll fix what was torn,
All I wanted was for us to be happy and never mourn.

Your voice played in my ear are pure sweet melodies,
It sparked my wanting to write you pretty symphonies,
I fight to stay in sanity and loosen your grip and bind,
But you're the only thing that keeps crossing my mind.

Why Do I Love You

I can't quite put a finger on when it happened,
When did I realise the glimmer in your eyes,
Intrigued by the way your mind works,
unfathomed,
It crept up oh so discreetly, this soul ties.

I can't quite figure out how it happened,
How you cracked the code to my guarded walls,
The way you walked through my fire unburned,
You had a way of patching up this broken doll.

I can't quite comprehend what happened,
What stringed the connection between us two,
What made you stay through changing seasons,
The colours you exude covered by mysterious
hue.

But I think I do know why it happened,
Why do I love you, or rather why I let you love me,
But they're reasons locked away in my heart's dungeon,
It's the only chained chamber where I hold the key.

When Love Crashed

The moment my ears took notice of your soft still voice,
I knew you would end up being my prime choice,
To make the fears disappear and my loneliness be gone,
It was found with you, with who I thought I belonged.

And now when others pay attention deep into my eyes,
They realised the tears I've shed, the tears I've cried,
From saying repeated hellos to never-ending goodbyes,
You can't blame me for feeling like I've lost my mind.

My mind wondered of how I should ask you to stay,
To make you entertain the feats I do, the words I say,
Till the day it hit me that you wouldn't be the one,
Till the day I realised my efforts are futile, I am done.

Seeing Me Through Your Eyes

You called me a plum blossom, winter flowers so rare,
Said that such beauty only blooms in adversity,
But I can't claim that label for myself, do I dare?
For I saw myself as nothing but chaff in the wind.

Still I try my best to grasp what you saw in me,
After all you've seen in me more than I ever could,
So I wrapped up what I loathe, all those flaws I see,
And tried to only display this "beauty" you had allude.

Yet the more I tried, the more I lost my speciality,
You did say the beauty appears not in the trying,
But in me just being me as natural as I can be,
So I returned to unwrap those flaws I had been fighting.

Turns out it's the battles that made my beauty
arise,
Such fragrance brought by harsh cold winter air,
I had no need to hide behind gentle mask or
disguise,
You loved me for my strength, raw and bare.

Forever Never Lasts

So I guess that truly turned out to be the last day,
That I would see the happiness of you walking my way,
This is a mistake, a slipup I will forever regret,
It's something I did I won't get to erase or forget.

But I can't use words to explain what I want to say,
I'm afraid you'd end up not bothered by me for days,
I wish you would've told me that you loved me too,
That you didn't end up standing behind playing cool.

I can't tell you how much I wish you were in my life,
The number of times I wish I could call you mine,
What I have now doesn't quite cut it, it's not enough,
I promise that all I wanted from you was just your love.

You Saw Through Me

All I had ever longed for was to be loved and found,
But I didn't dare show a hint of my desire for it,
I brushed aside the thought of bringing my walls down,
To take each layer down eventually brick by brick.

For I saw vulnerability as potential misguided arrows,
Aimed at my fragile heart when laid in the wrong hands,
So I buried myself deeper in my shielded up burrow,
Prepared for cuts and burns that I may come up against.

But you saw through my brave and bold façade,
Peeled off the layers and found someone precious,
Someone who had to put up the act of a stone-cold heart,
Someone whose heart remained soft under what appears.

You looked beyond the surface of my words and actions,
Knew that my true self was found in layers much deeper,
You saw through the core I held behind every intention,
That I truly bore a heart whether others knew any better.

Secret Wishes

I miss the times when you considered me your priority,
The times we shared still locked away in safekeeping,
For now to another's needs, I have become secondary,
Now for another, you keep caring, keep attending.

I was left as a castaway, a shell of emptiness ice cold,
With a fractured heart, all the more broken inside,
Why did you have to go afar and leave me here alone,
I knew I shouldn't have left you out of my sight.

Although I never let it show or let it be known,
But wherever you are, drop me your location and I'll go,
I miss the tenderness and gentleness you had shown,
Please don't leave me oblivious, don't leave me so.